D1502617

Let's Pray!

Everyday Prayers for Kids

For children who want to talk to God

Let's Pray!

Compiled by Su Box

Pictures by Leon Baxter

BROADMAN
& HOLMAN
PUBLISHERS

This collection copyright © 1998 Lion Publishing plc
Illustrations copyright © 1998 Leon Baxter
First North American edition published 1998
by Broadman & Holman Publishers
  127 Ninth Avenue, North
  Nashville, TN 37234

The author and artist have asserted their moral rights
to be identified as the author and artist of this work

Lion Publishing plc
Sandy Lane West, Oxford, England

ISBN 0-8054-1684-6

First edition 1998
10 9 8 7 6 5 4 3 2 1 0

All rights reserved

Acknowledgments
With thanks to the many children, parents and teachers
who helped with the creation of this book

A catalog record for this book is available
from the Library of Congress

Printed and bound in Malaysia

Contents

Contents

Introduction

The purpose of this book is to help young children take their first steps in prayer, so that talking to God becomes a natural everyday experience. These prayers are a starting-point – showing enjoyable and simple ways to give thanks and praise, to say sorry or to ask for God's help.

The prayers have been chosen to show that God is interested in every aspect of a child's life and that people can pray at any time and anywhere. Many of the prayers have been created by children themselves and show that you don't need special words to talk to God. In fact, talking to God can be just like talking to a loving parent or a best friend.

The book follows the pattern of a typical child's day, so you will find prayers to suit most moods and occasions. (A subject index offers additional direction to prayers on particular themes.)

You might like to ask your child to close their eyes as you read the words. Or they may prefer to look at the delightful pictures, which give added meaning to each prayer. Some of the prayers include suggestions for ways children can make a prayer their own (by saying the name of a friend or talking about a special experience), while others lend themselves to simple actions. And, of course, you can encourage children to join you in saying 'Amen' at the end of a prayer.

Before long, your child will have favorite prayers they want to return to again and again. But this book will also provide a first step toward a child's own prayers, helping him or her gain the confidence to share their own thoughts and feelings with God. This can be the first step of a lifelong friendship.

In the Morning

Waking Up

This morning, God,
This is your day.
I am your child,
Show me your way.
Amen

Thank you for each morning
I wake to a new day.
Thank you for my family,
For friends and fun and play.
Amen

You wake me up, God, to a new day.
Thanks to you I'm living.
Help me to live today as you wish.

A child's prayer

Thank you for this sunny morning.
It makes me happy.
Amen

Me

Lord, you know all about me...
I praise you because you made me
in an amazing and wonderful way.

From Psalm 139

God,
You made me,
You love me,
You look after me.
Thank you, God.

Dear God, Mom says I'm special.
Is it true there's no one else just like me?

A child's question

Dear God,
You know all about me:
The good things
and the bad things.
But you still think I'm special.
Thank you, God.

Let my thoughts and words
please you, Lord.
Amen

Two little eyes to look to God
Two little ears to hear his word,
Two little feet to walk in his ways,
Two little lips to sing his praise,
Two little hands to do his will,
And one little heart to love him still.

(This makes a good action rhyme.)

God, I can run and jump
and shout and SING!
I can skip and clap
and stamp and SWING!
Thank you for making me!

Family Times

I love them
And they love me,
Thank you for
My family.

Dear God, we've got a new baby!
He's* little and cries a lot.
When he's bigger I can play with him.
Thanks, God, for my new brother.

* Change throughout to suit a girl if necessary.

I'm sorry, God. I love my sister,*
but sometimes we fight.

* Change to suit a brother if necessary.

My prayer. God is good.
He gives us friends and family.
Amen

A child's prayer

Thank you for my Grandma
and her stories and cuddles.
Amen

Grandad takes me for walks.
He's very old. Please mend his bad knee.

Philip (aged 5)

Bless this house which is our home;
May we welcome all who come.

Meal Times

Each time we eat,
may we remember God's love.
Amen

A child's prayer

God is great;
God is good.
And we thank him
For our food.

For every cup and plateful
God make us truly grateful.

Thank you for the world so sweet,
Thank you for the food we eat.
Thank you for the birds that sing,
Thank you, God, for everything.

Dear God, thank you for all you give us.
Please help us to remember the needs
of others.
Amen

Through the Day

Playing

Loving God, on this day
Make us happy in our play,
Kind and helpful, playing fair,
Letting others have a share.
Amen

It's playgroup* day today!
Thank you, God.

* Change to whatever is appropriate for your child.

Dear God,
Thank you for making everything.
When I make something I think of you.
Amen

Dear God,
Thank you for painting and for
all the lovely colors. I'm glad you
don't mind if I make a mess!
Amen

Dear Lord
Thank you for friends
Thank you for the sea
Thank you for the world
And thank you for me.

Mark (aged 7)

Helping

Help me, God, to show how much I love
Mom and Dad by helping them.
Amen

Dear God, please look after me today
and help me to help others.
Amen

Dear God, I like to help, but I'm not
always good at it. Please help me to get
things right.
Amen

Thank you for the person who
helped me today.
Amen

My Friends

Thank you, God, for my friend*.
Please help me to be kind and share
my toys.

* Ask child to say the name of his or her friend.

Thank you for special friends
and games and secrets.
Amen.

Joseph (aged 5)

Dear God, I've been bad
And made my friend* sad.
Please help me to say sorry.

* Ask child to say the name of his or her friend.

Dear God, my friend* isn't well.
Please make him* feel better again.
Amen

* Ask child to say friend's name and substitute 'her' if necessary.

Thank you, God, for friends who care
when I'm feeling sad.
Thank you, God, for friends who share
and make me feel glad.

Lord, you are my best friend.
Thank you for all the things
you give to me.
Amen

Days Outside

Dear Lord on high,
Make a clear sky,
Make the day fine
And let the sweet sun shine.

Dear God,
It was fun in the park today.
Thank you for my friends and play.
Amen

For trees so tall
And flowers so small,
Thank you, God.
Amen

Hello, God, I like our world.
Thank you for making it.

Stephen (aged 4)

I'm sorry I was naughty at the store today.
Amen

A child's prayer

Dear God, thank you for cars, because
we can go a long way in them.

Gavin (aged 7)

Thank you for making the animals at the zoo and giving elephants big ears.
Amen

Ruth (aged 4)

Dear God, today we saw lots of wild
animals! Thank you for making so many
different kinds.
Amen

Weather

Thank you, God, for sunshine,
Thank you, God, for spring,
Thank you, God, for sending
Every lovely thing.

Dear God,
Please send lots of sun and showers
to help my seeds grow into flowers.
Amen

It's raining!
Rain makes our garden grow.
The ducks like rain.
Rain makes puddles I can jump in.
Thank you, God, for rain.

Thank you, God, for splashy puddles.
Amen

A child's prayer

Thank you, God, for making rainbows.
The lovely colors make me happy
on a wet day.

Amy (aged 5)

Dear God, please help me to remember
that you are bigger than the scary
thunder.
Amen

Thank you, God, for snowy days,
For those freezing, 'cold nose' days.
Amen

Thank you for the snowflakes,
Falling soft and white,
Making everything I see
Look clean and bright.

Animals

Thank you for the little ladybug
that sat on my finger today.
Amen

A child's prayer

Dear God, hear and bless
Your beasts and singing birds,
And guard with tenderness
Small things that have no words.

Dear God, can I tell you a secret?
I've got a new pet!*
Amen

A child's prayer

* Ask child to describe this new pet.

Dear God,
Thank you for my pets.* Please help
me to look after them and make them
feel loved.
Amen

* Ask child to name any family pets.

I like little puppies and kittens.
But why do they have to get big?
Amen

Luke (aged 5)

Dear God, my pet* has died.
I miss him so much. Please help me
to be happy again.
Amen

* Ask child to say pet's name.

Thank you for the cows that give us milk.

A child's prayer

Dear God, thank you for tadpoles.
I can't believe tadpoles turn into frogs.

Stephen (aged 3)

Dear God, thank you for giving the whale the big sea to swim in.

James (aged 5)

Happy Times

Today we're going to the seaside!
Thank you, God, that I can paddle in
the sea and play in the rock pools.
Amen

Thank you for summer:
For picnics
and ice cream.
It's fun in the sun!
Thanks God.

My lost teddy is back again.
Thank you, God.

Susie (aged 3)

Thank you for my Mom and Dad
and all the fun* we have together.
Amen

* Ask child to name experiences they have enjoyed.

Thank you, God,
for special days to look forward to
and special days to remember.
Amen

Thanks, God, for our vacation and all the
happy times we had.
Amen

Dear God, I just feel good knowing that
you are everywhere. That's all.

A child's prayer

I love you
my God!
I love you more than anything
in the world!
Praise to you, God.

Sad Times

I was sad today, God.
Thank you for being with me.
Amen

Thank you, God, for loving me,
even when I am cross.
Amen

Dear God, I am sick.
Thank you for the people
looking after me.
Please make me better.
Amen.

Dear God, please help my friend* be
happy when their mom or dad can't
be around.
Amen

* Ask child to name any friend they know in this situation.

I'm lonely, God.
Please help me to feel happy again.
Amen

My Grandmother* has died.
I won't see her anymore.
Mom says she's living with you now.
Please look after her.

* Substitute name as appropriate.

Dear God, knowing you are with me
when I'm sad is like knowing that the sun
is only hidden behind the clouds.
Amen

At Night

Quiet Times

Thank you for time
for a cuddle and a hug,
a time to share secrets
and feel safe and snug.
Amen

Thank you, God, for ears to hear.
When I'm quiet I can hear all sorts
of noises.*

* Ask child to listen and share what he or she can hear.

Thank you for the Bible. I like to hear stories about my friend Jesus.
Amen

Dear God, please help me to be quiet,
so that I can listen to you.
Amen

Bath Time

Thank you, God, for water
So that I can splash –
Having lots of bath time fun
As I wash.

Two eyes, two ears,
One mouth, one nose;
Fingers, tummy,
Knees and toes.
You made all these –
Thanks, God, for making me!

Bedtime

I go to bed and sleep in peace,
for you, Lord, keep me safe.

From Psalm 4

Bless my eyes
And bless my head,
Bless my dreams
Upon this bed.

Dear God, I like the twinkling stars.
But how do you keep them up?

A child's question

I see the moon
And the moon sees me.
God bless the moon,
And God bless me.

Dear God,
I'm sorry I was naughty today.
Please help me to be nice to Mom and
Dad tomorrow.
Amen

A child's prayer

Now that I lie down to sleep,
I ask you, Lord, your child to keep;
Your love be with me all the night,
And wake me with the morning light.

Dear God, when I wake up in the night
and feel afraid, please help me to
remember you are close beside me.
Amen

Special Days and Prayers

Birthdays

Today is my birthday, God!
Thank you for today and every day.

It's my birthday today.
Now I'm a year older,
help me to grow bigger
in a way that pleases you.
Amen

Dear Jesus, it's my birthday
and I am four* today.
Thank you for all the lovely things*
that make this a special day.
Amen

* Ask child to say their age and what makes today special for them.

Sunday

This is the day that the Lord has made.
Let us rejoice and be glad today!

From Psalm 118

Dear God,
I like it when we go to church,
We sing and then we pray.
We hear some Bible stories
And meet our friends and play.
Amen

Thank you for church and singing
and all my friends there.
Amen

A child's prayer

God, Sunday is your special day,
and I like it because Mom and Dad
don't make me 'hurry up'.

James (aged 5)

Christmas

Dear God, thank you for giving us your son, baby Jesus.
Amen

A child's prayer

Dear God,
Thank you for showing your love
by giving us the baby Jesus.
Help us to share Christmas love
everywhere.

Jesus, did you know we have a party
on your birthday?
It's because you were a special baby.
Can you come one year?

Daniel (aged 4)

Thank you, God, for Christmas surprises
And presents of all shapes and sizes.
For family and friends, and everyone
Who makes our Christmas Day such fun.
For special food and games to play
As we enjoy Jesus' birthday.

Easter

Thank you, God, that you love us
so much that you sent Jesus to die for us
so that we can be friends with you.
Amen

When Jesus died his friends were sad.
When Jesus rose his friends were glad.
I am happy too this Easter morning.

Dear Jesus, thank you for the new life
that Easter brings.
Amen

Dear Jesus, it hurt you on the cross.
But you got better, and you made
EVERYTHING better again.

Evie (aged 3)

The Lord's Prayer
(paraphrased for children)*

Our God,
We want you to be our King for ever:
then everyone will live as you want.
Give us each day all that we need.
Forgive us for the wrong things we do,
as we forgive people who hurt us.
Help us stop wanting to do bad things.
And keep us from all harm.
Amen

* Jesus loved to talk to God and pray. He taught his friends the
special prayer which we call 'The Lord's Prayer'.

Subject Index

Acknowledgments

Thanks go to all those who have given permission to include material in this book, as indicated in the list below. Every effort has been made to trace and contact copyright owners. We apologize for any inadvertent omissions or errors. All prayers except those acknowledged in the main text or listed below have been written by the author.

Pages 12 and 58: From *Children in Conversation with God.* Copyright © The Lutheran World Federation. Reproduced by kind permission of The Lutheran World Federation.

Pages 13, 25 and 36: From *The Infant Teacher's Prayer Book*, edited by Dorothy M. Prescott. Copyright © 1964 Blandford Press. Used by permission of Cassell plc.

Page 15: From *Prayers to Use with Under Fives* by Mary Bacon and Jean Hodgson. Published by the National Christian Education Council.

Page 19: By Colin C. Kerr, copyright © Mrs B. Kerr, from *CSSM Choruses, Book 1.*

Page 20: From *The Children's Book of Prayers*, compiled by Louise Carpenter. Copyright © 1988 Blackie and Sons Ltd.

Page 22: From *Talking to God* by Margaret Barfield. Copyright © 1997 Margaret Barfield. Published by Scripture Union.

Page 31: Copyright © 1959 and 1987 by Concordia Publishing House. Used with permission.

Pages 32, 52, 69, 85, 103 and 105 are all traditional prayers.

Page 33: From *Hymns and Songs for Children*. National Society.

Page 41: From *The Lion Prayer Collection*, compiled by Mary Batchelor. Copyright © 1992 Mary Batchelor. Published by Lion Publishing plc.

Pages 57 and 76: From *Children at Prayer*, edited by Rachel Stowe. Copyright © 1996 HarperCollins Publishers. Published by Marshall Pickering.

Page 60: From *My Own Book of Prayers*, compiled by Mary Batchelor. Copyright © 1984 Lion Publishing.

Pages 86 and 108: From *My First Prayer Book*. Copyright © Gwen Tansey and Cathy Jenkins. Used with permission of the publishers, HarperCollins Religious (Melbourne).

Page 99: Based on *Hello, Baby* by Felicity Henderson. Copyright © 1995 Lion Publishing.

Page 101: From *The Day I Fell Down the Toilet* by Steve Turner. Copyright © 1996 Steve Turner. Published by Lion Publishing plc.

ROCKVILLE PUBLIC LIBRARY

3 4035 11134 2768

J
MCA

McAllister, Angela.

Digory and the lost
king.

$14.95

DATE			

2c
2007
7/12 LC

CHILDREN'S DEPT.
Rockville Public Library
Vernon, CT 06066

BAKER & TAYLOR

BY ANGELA MCALLISTER & IAN BECK

Digory the Dragon Slayer

CHILDREN'S DEPT.
Rockville Public Library
Vernon, CT 06066

DIGORY

AND THE LOST KING

ANGELA MCALLISTER

illustrated by Ian Beck

BLOOMSBURY
CHILDREN'S
BOOKS

Text copyright © 2006 by Angela McAllister
Illustrations copyright © 2006 by Ian Beck
First published in Great Britain in 2006 by Bloomsbury Publishing Plc

All rights reserved. No part of this book may be used or reproduced
in any manner whatsoever without written permission from the publisher,
except in the case of brief quotations embodied in critical articles or reviews.

Published by Bloomsbury U.S.A. Children's Books
175 Fifth Avenue, New York, NY 10010
Distributed to the trade by Holtzbrinck Publishers

Library of Congress Cataloging-in-Publication Data
McAllister, Angela.
Digory and the lost king / Angela McAllister ; illustrated by Ian Beck.
p.   cm.
Summary: After having inadvertently acquired the reputation of being a brave young
knight, Digory, now also a prince living in the castle, goes in search of the missing
King Widget and finds his life complicated even further when he is mistaken for a
wizard.
ISBN-13: 978-1-59990-088-9 • ISBN-10: 1-59990-088-2 (hardcover)
ISBN-13: 978-1-59990-089-6 • ISBN-10: 1-59990-089-0 (paperback)
[1. Knight and knighthood—Fiction. 2. Wizards—Fiction.
3. Dragons—Fiction. 4. Humorous stories.] I. Beck, Ian, ill. II. Title.
PZ7.M47825Dil 2007   [Fic]—dc22   2006049941

First U.S. Edition 2007
Typeset by Polly Napper/Lobster Design
Printed in the U.S.A. by Quebecor World Fairfield
2 4 6 8 10 9 7 5 3 1 (hardcover)
2 4 6 8 10 9 7 5 3 1 (paperback)

All papers used by Bloomsbury U.S.A. are natural, recyclable products
made from wood grown in well-managed forests. The manufacturing processes
conform to the environmental regulations of the country of origin.

For Archie —A. M.

To Frances Holloway —I. B.

CONTENTS

Chapter One

HOW THINGS TURN OUT

IN days of old, when knights were bold, there lived a boy named Digory. He had lanky legs, red hair, and a nose like a sausage.

Digory came from a village called Batty-by-Noodle, where nothing much happened—and that's the way he liked it. All Digory wanted was to wander through the forest, wade around in streams, make up songs, and play his lute.

However, things don't always turn out the way we'd like. (Have you noticed?)

Somehow, Digory had been mistaken for a dragon-slaying hero and had been made a knight.

Somehow, he had been sent off on a deaf old carthorse named Barley to fight dragons and do noble deeds.

Somehow, despite running *away* from dragons, he had managed to do noble deeds anyway and been made a prince by grateful King Widget, who didn't have a prince of his own.

So, in days of old, when knights were bold, Prince Digory lived in Widget Castle, with the King, the Queen, and his best friend, Princess Enid. And he was just a bit older than you.

AN INVITATION

It was breakfast time at Widget Castle.

As usual, everything on the table had a label—coddled eggs, marigold pie, plum pudding, and dandelion juice. This was to help forgetful King Widget, who had trouble remembering the names of things.

The Queen also had a label, pinned to her robe. (In fact, she had a selection of labels to choose from: "Her Majesty" for when she was out and about in the realm, "She Who Must Be Obeyed" for when she was in a bad mood, and "Snugglepumpkin" for when she was alone with the King.)

"Now," said the Queen as she served everyone a royal-size portion of plum pudding, "is anything important happening this week?"

"Digory and I are going to make a nest for owls," said Enid.

"Oh, good," said the Queen.

"Enid and I are going to put a new roof on our treehouse," said Digory.

"Oh, good," said the Queen.

"And I've organized a bit of a whatsit," said the King.

"Oh, dear!" The Queen sighed.

"Yes," said the King, "we're going to have . . . um . . . oh, you know . . ."

"What *kind* of thing are we going to have?" asked Enid. "Animal, vegetable, or mineral?"

"Animal? Yes, animals—lots of 'em," said the King happily.

Digory's heart sank. He hoped these animals weren't dragons. Once before, the King had sent him on an errand to slay a dragon, which had resulted in a very uncomfortable adventure. (Digory still wasn't sure what had actually happened. He knew he'd tried to trick the dragon, chased it, run away from it, nearly been gobbled up by it, flown on its back, *actually* been gobbled up by it, mysteriously escaped, and . . . well . . . somehow the dragon had disappeared.)

Digory was certain that he never wanted to see another dragon ever, ever again.

"Is it a hamster, Your Majesty?" he asked hopefully.

"Hamster! Ha ha!" the King roared with laughter. "No, no, no, Diggers. It's a . . . a . . . charge-and-thrust!" He stabbed at the air with an imaginary weapon. "It's a strike-and-blow, a bump-and-tumble!"

Suddenly Enid jumped up and ran out of the breakfast chamber. A moment later she returned carrying a broom.

"I know!" She took up the reins of an imaginary pony, lowered the broomstick, and began galloping up and down the room.

"Oh, yes!" cried the Queen, clapping her hands with glee. "Of course . . . it's a joust!

Clever girl."

"That's it!" The King beamed.

Enid dropped the broom and flung her arms around her father.

"Haven't had one for ages," said the King. "Used to joust with my brother . . . um . . ."

"Wortle," said the Queen.

"Bless you," said the King.

"No, Wortle—it's your brother's name. King Wortle."

"Oh, yes, so it is—or at least it *was*," said the King mysteriously. He heaved a great sigh and a sudden sadness overcame the whole family. They fell silent.

Digory was puzzled. He had never heard of King Wortle before. Why did the mention of his name make everyone so sad?

Before Digory had a chance to ask, Cook arrived with a bowl of plump, shiny strawberries, which stirred everyone out of their gloomy mood.

"As I was saying," muttered the King, helping himself to the fattest fruit, "Wortle and I

15

always used to get together and organize some fun and games the week before our birthday, Diggers. You know, invite the whole village and the next-door-nosy-nobles around."

"Daddy and Wortle are twins," whispered Enid in Digory's ear.

"But we haven't done it in a while." A royal frown crumpled King Widget's brow. The Queen quickly handed him another strawberry. "Anyway," the King continued, "the birthday's coming up and since we've got Digory here now, I thought we'd have a . . . whatever it is . . . broom-bashing."

16

"Joust, Daddy, joust!" squealed Enid.

"Just what I was thinking," said the King. "I set one up for Saturday. Shouldn't be a problem for a young prince like you, Diggers. Too old for it myself these days. Great fun, yes. Charge and thrust, charge and thrust!"

Digory's breakfast turned to stone in his tummy. "But I don't know how to joust, Your Majesty," he protested.

"Plenty of time for practice," said the King. "It's only Wednesday today. Practice makes perfect, Digory my lad."

And that was the end of that.

Well, that wasn't the end of that. It was just the beginning for Prince Digory.

PRACTICE MAKES PERFECT

Poor Digory went off to the stables to tell Barley the bad news.

Barley, his deaf old carthorse, knew as

much about jousting as Digory did. She adopted Digory's unhappy mood and chewed her gums in a what-about-retiring-me-to-a-quiet-meadow? sort of way.

Digory, ignoring her silent plea, sat on an upturned bucket and composed a song called "I'd Rather Eat Hay Than Be Knocked Off My Bay." That was how Enid found him.

Enid always understood Digory. She was the first true friend he'd ever had. She wasn't huffy and proud like the other princesses Digory had met doing his noble deeds. She didn't sit in a tower all day, combing her long, golden hair. She didn't even *have* long, golden hair—hers was mud brown and stuck up like a hedgehog. She liked to wander through the forest, wade around in streams, climb trees, and play her krummhorn. Enid, you see, was an unusual sort of princess and had a lot in common with Digory, who was an unusual sort of knight. Best of all, she always had a smile and a good idea.

"Cheer up," she said, giving Barley a bite of her apple. "It won't be so bad, Digory. I'll help you practice for the joust."

"But I don't want to knock you off your horse with a stick," sighed Digory. "I might hurt you. In fact, I don't want to knock anyone off his horse."

"It's not a stick, it's a lance," laughed Enid, "and that's the point of a jousting tournament. You have to topple your opponent or he'll topple you first."

Digory had no doubt at all that he was going to wake up on Sunday morning covered in bumps and bruises.

"Try *pretending* to be fierce and competitive," said Enid, "even if you don't feel it. Just start by pretending. You might surprise yourself."

Digory thought of his bold brothers, Arthur and Tom. They really *were* fierce and competitive. They competed over who could chop firewood the fastest, who could trap the biggest boar, even who could stuff the most crumpets into his mouth at once.

And Digory's sister, Ethelburg, captain of the Mucky Maidens' Mudflinging Team, was fierce and competitive too. No one was fiercer than Ethelburg when her team was losing, as she thundered toward her opponents like a mud tempest, with flashing wild eyes and bloodcurdling shrieks.

Even Digory's mother, Betsy the blacksmith, competed each year in the local hammer-tossing championship and remained unbeaten.

But Digory wasn't like that.

"There's room for all kinds, son," his dad used to say. "Just be yourself."

But there's room for only one kind at a joust, thought Digory, *and it's definitely the fierce, competitive kind.* Maybe pretending *was* the only way. He looked at Enid's excited face.

"All right, I'll try," he said with a heavy heart.

"I knew you would!" said Enid, tweaking his nose.

At these words Barley stamped a hoof disapprovingly, as if maybe she wasn't quite so deaf after all . . .

So began Digory's apprenticeship in jousting. For the rest of the week he cantered around the tilting yard on Barley, stabbing a lance at a sack stuffed with straw. Enid never ran out of encouraging words, but by Friday night she had a sore throat from shouting so much, and Digory hadn't hit the sack once!

"If only we had more time to train," croaked Enid. "It's just a matter of balance and timing . . ."

"And aim and strength, and horsemanship and bravery," groaned Digory. "Not much to master in three days! If only it was a sword fight instead." Digory had been given a magic sword by an unreliable wizard named Burdock. (The magic always took some time to warm up, but the sword had turned out to be quite useful.)

"That wouldn't be fair," said Enid.

"I don't think the joust will be fair either," said Digory. "Everyone else will be much better than I am."

Even Enid couldn't argue with that. But as we have noticed before, things don't always turn out the way you expect . . .

TIME TO PRETEND

On the morning of the joust, King Widget woke up with a terrible case of the sneezes.

"Oh, what a pity," sighed the Queen, plumping up his pillows. "I'm afraid you'll have to stay at home."

"Bodder!" grumbled the King. "Ah don't want to mith the j . . . j . . . j'atishoo!"

"I'll send for hot soup and hot-water bottles and hankies and jigsaw puzzles," said the Queen. "Maybe, if you feel a little better this afternoon, you could watch from the battlements. But now I can hear the tent poles being hammered into the green. I'm afraid I have to go and make sure Digory has a very good breakfast." And she bustled off to fuss over the cook.

The Queen had ordered up a great feast to start the day. But poor Digory had no appetite. He sat at the breakfast table, staring at his plate. Two fried eggs and a sausage jeered at him with a mocking grin. Digory's tummy turned somersaults and wouldn't settle down, not even for a sausage with a doubtful sense of humor.

Enid, however, had been watching the tournament preparations since dawn, and she was excited enough to eat for two.

Digory secretly slid his breakfast into his napkin, so as not to disappoint the Queen. Then he slipped away to prepare Barley.

At the stable, however, Digory discovered that the old horse had somehow gotten wind of the galloping and poking that was soon to take place and had stubbornly turned her back to the door, refusing to budge. It took four squires and a handful of peppermints to persuade her out.

Meanwhile, guests began to arrive from every corner of the kingdom. Bold knights galloped around the moat, impatient to begin the competition. Damsels tried to distract them by getting into distress all over the place. Flags fluttered, muffin men strolled among the gaily colored tents, and the village children found plenty of mischief.

Digory put on his cold, clammy armor. It

25

made him shiver so much, his teeth rattled. He remembered how proud his mother had been the day she made it for him. *She really believed I was brave enough to slay a dragon*, he thought as he pulled on his gauntlets.

Then Digory looked at Enid, who had come to give his tin boots one last polish. She believed he was brave too—brave enough to joust for the King. And curiously, as he considered this, Digory's teeth stopped rattling and he warmed up a little inside. (I'm sure you know that when someone believes in you, your heart swells like a sun-ripe peach. And that's bound to warm you up a bit, isn't it?)

When all his straps were strapped and his buckles buckled, Digory was hoisted onto Barley's back. Enid gave the old carthorse a good-luck carrot.

"Remember," she whispered to Digory as she handed him his lance and shield, "remember to pretend . . ."

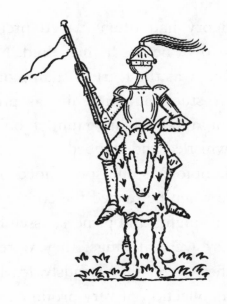

Chapter Two

THE NEVER-ENDING JOUST

As Digory plodded out into the sunshine, the sweet smell of muffins hit his nose and the local villagers began to cheer. With this encouragement, he tried a fierce and competitive smile. The crowd cheered louder. *This is not so bad*, Digory thought. As usual, Enid was right. Maybe he just had to pretend after all. Digory had often played pretend games on his own before he met Enid. Now he imagined he was the fearless champion of the joust. He stuck out his chin, as proud knights do, and waved his gauntlet boldly. The crowd whistled and clapped.

But the champion's smile soon faded from Digory's face when he turned the corner and saw the other knights and princes, assembled together. They were all huge, they were all bold, and they were all obviously fearless! (And what a collection of very proud chins!)

Now, to add to his sudden terror, Digory was told that he was to go last. Poor Digory had to wait and watch the rest of the knights pulverize each other. Knocked sideways, armor crumpled, and bones broken, they fell to the ground, groaning, and were carried away to the first-aid tent.

As the last pair of knights trotted forward to tilt their lances to the Queen, Digory bent down and whispered in Barley's ear. "I think I'll pretend to be someone else now, someone who lives in the next kingdom . . ." And he gently pulled her reins to lead her quietly away.

But Digory had the unusual habit of always arriving at the place he was trying to avoid. As he and Barley emerged from the maze of tall tents, a great cheer erupted and there they were—facing the crowd.

"Hooray for Prince Digory!" yelled the local villagers.

"Digory the champion!"

A plowman's boy ran up and tied a ribbon onto Barley's rein. The Queen smiled down from her garden throne nearby and said, "Good luck, Digory, dear. Remember what the King said—charge and thrust."

Enid, sitting beside her mother, screwed up her face and made a fierce expression. Digory understood. He summoned all his pretending-power to feel like a jousting champion, but he could feel only like quivering jelly.

"Oh well, Barley," he said. "Here we go."

Digory pulled down his visor. Inside the dark helmet he suddenly had one last, desperate hope. Maybe he would wake up and find it was just a terrible dream after all . . .

THE FEARSOME FOE

But Digory didn't wake up.

Drums rolled. The crowd hushed.

"Step forward, Prince Digory of Widget Castle," bellowed the local butcher, who was announcing things, "and Lord Percy of Rosebud Manor."

At the other end of the field Digory's opponent stepped forward. To Digory's amazement, Lord Percy was small and thin. Even his armor had knobby knees. His horse, which looked suspiciously like a pony, was old and shabby. Digory guessed that both horse and rider knew as little about jousting as he and Barley did.

For once Digory was right.

With a fanfare of trumpets, the joust began.

Lord Percy's horse strolled over to the near-est flag and began to eat it.

Barley sat down.

Lord Percy dismounted and tugged his horse back to the start.

Digory dismounted and gave Barley a big nudge.

Lord Percy and Digory, in their heavy armor, had to be hoisted onto their chargers all over again.

Lord Percy lowered his lance and promptly fell off.

Digory lowered his lance and got it tangled up in his reins. Then he fell off.

The crowd collapsed in fits of laughter. It seemed Digory *had* been fairly matched after all.

The joust continued like this for three hours. Lord Percy broke four lances and two sets of reins and charged into the first-aid tent, scattering spectators over the nearest hedge.

Digory broke three lances, lost a tin boot, and snagged the royal tent ropes, bringing the whole tent down like a parasol.

The Queen and her guests recovered while the tent was put up again. Then the combat had to go on because there was still no winner—and the rules of the tournament said there had to be a winner, one way or another.

"Let the combat proceed," bellowed the butcher. "Now with swords!"

"No. I don't think that's wise," said the Queen. "Let's go straight to fisticuffs."

"Fisticuffs!" yelled the butcher.

Digory hadn't practiced this. But neither, it seemed, had Lord Percy.

Lord Percy swung out and hit himself on the chin.

Digory tried to wallop Lord Percy, who ducked, and hit himself on the head.

Lord Percy dodged like a flitting butterfly, stepped back, and fell over his exhausted horse.

Digory ran forward, fists waving madly in the air, and tripped over his own lost boot.

And so the fisticuffs match went on—for two hours.

At Last . . .

At last a cart carrying a small barrel was wheeled up.

Thank goodness, thought Digory, who was hot and thirsty, *a barrel of water*.

"Conkers!" bawled the butcher, and he threw Digory and Lord Percy a ball of string. Sure enough, the barrel was full of horse chestnuts of all shapes and sizes, helpfully drilled with holes.

Digory's heart sank.

Lord Percy's heart sank.

But there had to be a winner.

Digory and Lord Percy chose their chestnuts
and threaded them onto strings.

Once more they faced each other.

Once more the crowd held its breath. (Well,
the part of the crowd that hadn't given up
and gone home. The part of the crowd still
left that hadn't gone to sleep.)

Lord Percy bent forward and whispered.

"Should we run away? There's maypole dancing over in the next kingdom."

Digory thought for a moment: *Maypole dancing, music, caramel apples, sitting on a grassy bank, watching the fair. What a great idea.* Then he saw Enid, still making fierce, competitive faces to spur him on.

"No," sighed Digory, not quite able to hide his regret. For Enid's sake, he attempted a fearful scowl. "Raise your conker, you . . . you stinker!"

Thwack! Lord Percy swung his chestnut and it whizzed off its string, hurtled straight through the castle window, bounced off the kitchen wall, and plopped into the cooking pot, splashing the cook with custard.

"Oh, dear," sighed the Queen with a yawn, "something tells me we could be here until bedtime."

And she was right.

There followed two hours of conker bonking. Chestnuts flew perilously at the few loyal spectators left. Chestnuts splashed into the lake, terrifying the swans, and broke every window on that side of the castle. Digory and Lord Percy were dented all over, with fine black eyes each.

Still there was no winner between them.

When a chestnut landed, bull's-eye, on the butcher's bald head, he decided enough was enough.

"Tiddlywinks!" he bellowed.

"Thank goodness," sighed the Queen. Now, she knew this was one sport that Digory had practiced very well, as the whole family loved to play tiddlywinks by the fire on winter evenings. But, as luck would have it, so did Lord Percy's family.

Two hours later, Baron Squinteye, who was sitting behind the Queen, leaned forward and whispered in her ear. "Might I mention, Your Majesty, for the future, that tiddlywinks is not much fun to watch." He peered down at Digory and Lord Percy flipping their tiny counters across an upturned barrel. "They're so, well, they're so *tiddly*!"

But the Queen just muttered "Fluff 'n' fiddlestuff." For she too had finally nodded off to sleep.

Snnnrrrrgh . . .

Digory and Lord Percy played tiddlywinks until twilight. Still there was no winner between them.

By the time they had eventually lost the last tiddlywink in the grass, even the butcher had gone home, hoping his greedy family had left a chop for his dinner.

"How should we compete now?" asked Digory.

"First one home?" suggested Lord Percy.

"Musical statues!" shouted one person in the crowd.

"Loudest burps!" shouted the other person in the crowd.

"Stuffing the most ferrets down your pants," said a poacher (busy stuffing as many leftover muffins as he could down his).

"I know," said Enid wearily, "what about thumb wrestling?" As this was a sitting-down sort of sport, Digory and Lord Percy agreed. They clamped their fists together.

"Repeat after me," said Enid. "One, two, three, four. I declare a thumb war. Stand, bow, fight!"

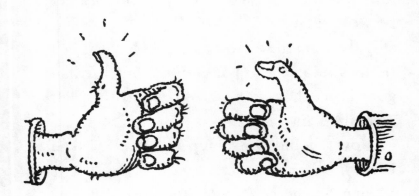

The thumbs stood, bowed, and fought. And for such little guys, it was a furious combat.

Digory had superior strength from playing the lute, but Lord Percy had some nifty moves.

"Hup!"

"Ha!"

"Oi!"

"Ow!"

It was all over in a minute. Lord Percy's

thumb fell, stunned, onto his palm. Digory's delighted digit wiggled triumphantly!

"I've won!" he cried. "I've won at last!" Digory creaked to his feet and raised his champion thumb to the crowd . . . but no one cheered. The last two spectators had left with the poacher to eat the muffins, and everyone else had fallen asleep or gone home.

Lord Percy, nursing his defeated warrior, stumbled off to his tent, just pleased that it was all over.

Only Enid remained to congratulate Digory. "Well done," she said proudly. "I knew you could do it. Now, let's wake Mom and all go home to bed."

At the sound of the word "bed," Digory yawned happily. How he got there he never remembered.

Chapter Three

LOST KINGS

WHEN the Queen, Enid, and Digory returned to the castle after the tournament that evening, the King had already gone to bed.

"Poor dear Widgey," sighed the Queen. "An early night will do him good." She decided not to disturb him and slept in the spare bedchamber instead.

The next morning everyone slept late. In fact, nobody got up for breakfast at all. It wasn't until the smell of roasting parsnips wafted up the spiral staircase that the Queen, Enid, and Digory got up for lunch.

"I hope the King remembered to have some dinner last night," fretted the Queen. "His forgetfulness has gotten much worse recently."

"He hasn't forgotten his birthday on Friday," said Enid. "He *never* forgets that. I want to give him the best present in the whole world."

"The best present in the whole world would be a visit from his brother, King Wortle," said the Queen. Once more Digory noticed the Queen and Enid grow sad at the mention of King Wortle's name.

"What's wrong?" Digory asked. "Why don't we just invite him? It must be King Wortle's birthday too."

"That *is* what's wrong," said Enid. "King Wortle disappeared from his home, Claggy-boot Castle, on his birthday ten years ago and hasn't been seen since."

"King Widget misses him so much," said the Queen. "They were best friends, you see, as well as brothers."

Digory looked at his own best friend, Enid. He remembered how awful he felt when the dragon, Horrible Gnasher Toast'em Firebreath, wanted to gobble her up for breakfast. How unhappy he would be if she disappeared and was never seen again.

"We'll have to think of something very special for Daddy's birthday to cheer him up," said Enid. "Maybe a piglet race? He likes a nice, squealy piglet race—the squeakier the better."

Cook arrived with the roasted parsnips.

"Have you seen the King?" asked the Queen.

"No, Your Majesty," Cook replied. "He didn't have any dinner and he didn't have any breakfast and it doesn't look as if he wants any lunch, either!"

"That's unusual," said the Queen. "He must be feeling worse." She put four of the crispiest, most golden parsnips on the King's plate.

"I'll see if I can tempt him myself." And off she went to find him.

While the Queen was gone, Enid and Digory began to plan the piglet race.

"Let's give them a nice mud bath at the end," said Digory.

"And tubs of turnips," said Enid, "and . . ."

Suddenly the Queen flew through the doorway, her wimple streaming and her face as white as milk.

"The King is gone!" she cried. "*He has disappeared!*"

Chapter Four

FORGETFULNESS

EVERYONE in the castle, from the black-smith to the dairymaid, hunted for King Widget. Digory searched the King's favorite snoozing places. Enid knew the secret haunts where her father liked to hide when the Queen had a list of things for him to do. But he wasn't to be found in any of them.

"No one saw him leave the castle," sobbed the Queen. "He just disappeared, like his brother—and with the sneezes!"

Enid comforted her mother. "Maybe he left a clue somewhere."

The Queen got the King's diary. "This will tell us what was on his mind . . ."

King Widget liked to keep a diary. It helped him to remember things.

The Queen read it aloud:

"Monday.
Ruled all day. Decided to organize a charge-and-thrust.
Tuesday.
Ruled all day. Lost bedslippers.
Wednesday.
Ruled all morning. Went for a walk. Found one of W's old chessmen in the juice-drippy-munch-place. Missed W.
Thursday.
Took the day off. Forty winks under squeak-squeak-bang. Missed W.

Friday.
Watched E and D play hoop-and-tortoise.
Found bedslippers in cat's basket.
P. S. Must visit W."

"What does it all mean?" puzzled Digory.

"W . . . ," said Enid. "That must be Wortle."

"And the juice-drippy-munch-place might be the orchard," suggested Digory. "But squeak-squeak-bang?" None of them could guess until they heard a familiar racket outside—the sound of the drawbridge being lowered. Each turn of the chain wheel made an excruciating squeak. Then the bridge hit the ground with a loud thud and a "cock-a-doodle-do" as the rooster made off without his tail feathers.

"Aha," muttered the Queen, *"that's* where he was when I wanted to visit Mother on Thursday."

"Do you think he went to find King Wortle?" Digory wondered.

"It does look as though he forgot that his

brother disappeared," said Enid. "He must have gone off to Claggyboot Castle."

"All by himself and with the sneezes!" gasped the Queen. "Digory, dear, you are the prince. You must find him at once. And take him a clean handkerchief."

Now, Digory had been asked to do many things he thought he couldn't do (and been made to do some things he wished he hadn't done), but he jumped up at once, like a true prince, to rescue the King.

"I'll find him, Your Majesty," he said, secretly sliding a couple of roasted parsnips into his pocket in case he wasn't back for dinner. "I promise. I won't return without him."

"Then I'm coming too," said Enid. "I'll pack a picnic and saddle up my pony."

Digory smiled gratefully and sneaked the parsnips back.

Before you could say "royal rescue," Enid had saddled up her pony, Flibbertigibbet, and Barley too. Digory brought the picnic basket, the magic sword, and a map to show them the way to Claggyboot Castle. And, with a reassuring wave to the Queen, they trotted over the drawbridge.

THE SOGGY SEARCH

Digory and Enid traveled along a river, through the greenwood, over a small hill, over a large hill, and up a mountain path. Here, in unfamiliar territory, they stopped to look at the map.

Digory had dealt with maps before.

"Are you sure it's the right way up?" he asked Enid as she studied it closely.

"Yes," said Enid. "Look, there's *N* for north at the top."

"But how do you know which way north is?" asked Digory.

"Because that's the way the map is pointing," replied Enid confidently. Digory, very

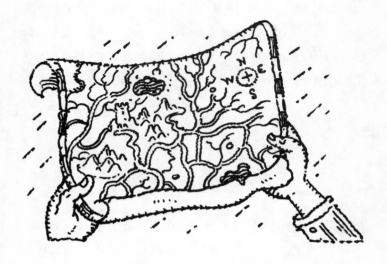

happy to leave the directions to someone else, decided not to ask any more questions.

A wind shook the trees and the sky darkened.

I do hope the King has arrived somewhere, Digory thought, *wherever he has gone.*

"Look, here's Claggyboot Castle," Enid pointed to a small inky picture of a tower, "at the end of the valley on the other side of this mountain." But as Digory peered at the map, the tower mysteriously melted away before their eyes, leaving nothing but a blue smudge.

"Oh, no, it's a magic map!" gasped Digory. "Or else . . ." Cautiously he raised his head to see if there were a wizard leaning over their shoulders making mischief. Splat! A fat raindrop smacked him in the eye.

Enid hurriedly rolled up the parchment before the whole map was washed away and stuffed it inside her tunic. "We'd better look for shelter," she said.

Thunder rolled and the mountain echoed back with a growl. Black, grumpy clouds crowded the sky, looking for a big, wet fight.

Digory spotted a cave in the mountainside. "That should be large enough for all of us."

Suddenly a spear of lightning stabbed the sky. Flibbertigibbet got a fright and reared up, sending Enid tumbling onto the grass. Then, with a whinny, the scatterbrained pony bolted off down the path, taking the picnic with her!

At that moment the big, rainy cloud fight began. Digory, Enid, and Barley made a dash for the cave.

"Are you hurt?" asked Digory.

"Oh, no." Enid grinned and rubbed her bruises. "I'm used to that. But I do hope Daddy is out of the rain . . ."

Digory and Enid sat and watched the storm all afternoon. They played "I Spy" and sang songs to keep their spirits up. Barley settled herself at the back of the cave.

Soon an eerie rumble echoed around them. Enid stared nervously over her shoulder. She wondered if there were a tunnel in the darkness behind them. "Do you think there are sleeping dragons in this mountain?" she whispered.

"I don't think so." Digory blushed. "That's my hunger-rumble!" But the picnic had galloped away—what could they eat? Digory wished he had kept those roasted parsnips he'd smuggled into his pocket at lunch. He decided to try and brew up some soup.

Digory knew all about edible herbs and roots from his days spent rambling in the woods around Batty-by-Noodle. He gathered what he could find near the cave entrance and put them into his helmet, which he filled with rainwater. Being the son of a blacksmith, he also knew how to light a good fire. However, even the best blacksmith needed dry sticks. Digory's were all wet.

"Why don't you try the magic sword?" suggested Enid. Digory heaped up the sticks and pointed the sword at them. Nothing happened. They waited. Nothing happened again. But this was the sort of magic sword it was—slow and not very enthusiastic. Then, like a glimmer of hope, a tiny speck of light began to glow deep in the wet bundle. Slowly it grew into a little red tongue that began to lick those sticks, and to Digory and Enid's delight, there was soon a crackling fire and a helmet full of bubbling broth.

After their cheering meal of soup, followed by a handful of damp blackberries and hazelnuts, Enid and Digory tried to use the sword to make the storm move along to the next mountain. But sadly, as they'd expected, the magic was not strong enough for that. The rainstorm continued on into the evening, until there was nothing left to do but stoke the fire, make themselves comfortable, and spend the night in the cave.

THINGS THAT GO CRACK
IN THE NIGHT . . .

Digory had a happy dream that King Widget was sleeping in the same cave and they were all reunited in the morning.

Well, there was someone sleeping at the back of the cave that night—or at least some*thing*.

As Enid had feared, there *was* a tunnel in the darkness behind them. And at the other end of that tunnel, deep under the mountain, was a great cavern. And in that cavern, on a nest of bones, was a large egg. And in that

egg was something fast asleep, waiting to be born . . .

In the middle of the night, the egg started to crack. Out popped a tiny claw. Then another. Out peeped a tiny green eye.

A little dragon pushed her horny head through the shell and looked around for her mother. But her mother wasn't there—she was twenty leagues away, chomping on a poor, unfortunate maiden who'd been riding home at twilight wearing very flashy jewels.

The baby dragon sniffed the air. A wisp of smoke drifted into the cavern from the mouth of a tunnel nearby.

Now, to a fire-breathing dragon, a whiff of smoke is very comforting. She clambered out of the egg, stretched her trembling wings, and shuddered. The cavern was cold and empty. So she set off along the tunnel toward the source of the smoke, hoping to find her mother . . .

Chapter Five

A MORNING SURPRISE

BARLEY opened one eye. A beam of morning light danced between her ears. So far so good.

But other things weren't quite right. She was not in her stable. She was not sitting on comfy straw. And something told her she was probably not going to get a feedbag of sweet hay for breakfast.

Something else was wrong. Nuzzled up beside her, with its head buried in her mane, was a small dragon. Barley opened the other eye.

The baby dragon, feeling the old carthorse stir, lifted its face to Barley's, blinked happily, and licked her nose.

Barley had never had a foal of her own. Thinking about this arrangement for a moment, she decided it felt good. So she nestled her new baby closer and went back to sleep.

POUNCE

Enid woke Digory with the good news that the sun was shining. "And look what I found in my pocket this morning," she said. "A bag of bramble jelly beans! They're a bit squashed but they'll make a good breakfast, and then we must be on our way. Do you think Barley could carry us both?"

"D-d-d-," stuttered Digory.

"Are you cold?" asked Enid.

"D-d-d-," repeated Digory.

"Is it a game?" asked Enid. "Something beginning with *d*? Can't we have breakfast first?"

"D-d-d-" Digory raised his shaking hand and pointed toward Barley.

"Oh! DRAGON!" squealed Enid.

Digory grabbed Enid's hand and pulled her out of the cave. They made a dive for the nearest bush and scrambled beneath it, out of sight.

Enid and Digory whispered fiercely under the bush.

"We have to wake up Barley!"

"How can we do that without waking up the dragon?"

"Do you think it's big enough to eat Barley?"

"No."

"Do you think it's big enough to eat us?"

"No."

"Do you think it's big enough to breathe fire?"

A sudden flicker of sparks at the back of the cave answered that question. The dragon's fiery sigh had set Barley's mane on fire. Digory scrambled out from under the bush, ran into the cave, grabbed his helmet, and threw the rest of the cold soup on Barley's head. Horse and dragon woke up with a start.

Enid peered out from under the bush in terror. Digory stood, frozen to the spot.

Barley, shaking the soup from her ears,

staggered to her feet and ambled out into the sunshine. The little dragon followed.

Barley found a patch of long grass and began to help herself to breakfast. The little dragon watched for a moment and did the same.

Barley stamped her hoof and twitched her tail. So did the little dragon.

Then, as Digory and Enid watched in astonishment, Barley lay down and rolled in the warm grass and the little dragon tumbled playfully beside her.

"That dragon thinks Barley is her mother!" said Enid. And so she did.

Digory and Enid soon saw they were in no danger of being eaten by their new friend, but neither could they separate the little dragon from her adopted mother.

"Well, either we leave Barley behind with the dragon and continue on foot," Digory said to Enid, "or we take her with us."

There was really no choice. After a quick

look at the map, Digory and Enid both climbed onto Barley's back and set off once more along the mountain path, with the little dragon tagging along behind.

The dragon was easily distracted by birds and butterflies and even by her own tail, which she leaped on whenever it swung into view. So they named her Pounce and everyone, especially proud Barley, was delighted with their new traveling companion.

Digory was also distracted by anything that flew into view—but for a different reason. He was worried that Pounce's real mother might return at any moment and mistake them for dragon-nappers . . .

ON THE KING'S TRAIL

Digory was relieved when, at last, they left the open mountain path and took a shady track along the edge of a forest. *At least we'll be able to dive into the wood if any trouble comes along*, he told himself. Still, he watched the sky warily. "If only we had a disguise for Pounce," he muttered.

At these words, a brown cloak fell from a branch above and landed on the little dragon's head. Pounce gave a snort of surprise and set fire to it.

In the sudden confusion, a long stick and net also fell out of the tree, followed by a wide-brimmed hat and a plump, red-faced man, who clambered down after them, puffing and panting. He pulled the cloak off Pounce at once and stamped on the flames.

"Smoldering stitches!" he cried. "You can't just go around setting fire to a fellow's cloak like that. I'll be shivering all winter! Mrs. Buzz will have to patch it up with bee fur."

Mr. Buzz, as you might guess, was a beekeeper.

"Well, what were you doing up in that tree?" asked Digory.

"Looking for my bees," he said. "Though

all this fuss will have scared them off to Timbuktu!"

Enid looked closely at Mr. Buzz's smoking cloak. Scarlet threads showed through here and there. Sure enough, it wasn't brown at all, but red cloth covered in mud. "This is the King's cloak!" she cried excitedly.

"Nonsense!" said Mr. Buzz. "It's my very own."

"My father, the King, has disappeared," explained Enid. "Prince Digory and I have come to look for him. This cloak may give us a clue."

Mr. Buzz sat down on his hat in disbelief. Digory and Enid hadn't noticed that, after being caught in the rain and sleeping in a cave, they didn't look like a prince and princess at all. "How do I know you aren't clever cloak-thieves?" asked Mr. Buzz suspiciously.

Digory, who was already feeling like a guilty dragon-napper, thought this was very unfair. "We don't want to steal anything," he said. "We want to find the King." Suddenly he had an idea. "Look inside the collar," he said. "The King always has the name of things sewn into his clothes."

Sure enough, when Mr. Buzz looked inside the collar, he found a label the Queen herself had stitched, saying "Cloak."

Mr. Buzz looked very bashful. "Your Majesties, Your Most Royal Highnesses." He bowed to Enid and Digory. "I never knew it was the King's cloak. I bought it yesterday from Truffle, the pig man," he said. "Paid him two honest shillings."

"Then I'll give you two shillings for it," said Enid, "if you tell us how to find him."

Mr. Buzz told them the way through the woods to Truffle's cottage. "You'll know when you're getting close . . . ," he said mysteriously. "And if you see my bees, just send them home."

They set off through the woods and Digory wondered how he might explain to a swarm of bees that it was time to go home. He was still pondering the danger and difficulty of this when his nose suddenly told him that Truffle's cottage was near. As the pig smell grew stronger, they heard a scurry of little hooves among the bushes. They found Truffle emptying a sack of apples into his cart.

"Fine morning," said Truffle shyly. He offered an apple to Barley but nearly jumped out of his skin when Pounce appeared from behind her, neighing hungrily. (She'd been quick to pick up Barley's voice as well as her habits.)

"Could you give her an apple too, please?" asked Digory. "She thinks she's a horse."

Truffle stuck an apple on the end of a stick and offered it to Pounce at arm's length.

Enid saw how nervous he was and asked quickly about her father's cloak.

"I got it from Clod, the well-digger," said Truffle. "Paid him one honest shilling too."

Digory thanked him and bought enough apples to fill their saddlebag. Then on they went to the village where Clod the well-digger lived.

To their dismay, Clod the well-digger had no news about King Widget. "I got it down at the market, from Nell the stocking-maker," he said. "Paid her an honest sixpence."

Digory and Enid tramped on to the market square.

Naughty Nell pretended she'd made the cloak herself. But when Enid showed her the label, Nell admitted she'd gotten it from Crust the baker.

They found Crust the baker, who said he'd gotten it from Botch the carpenter.

They found Botch the carpenter, who said he'd gotten it from Slurp the slop-bucket boy.

They found Slurp, who wouldn't say a word about the cloak until Digory warned him he had a magic sword—then Slurp burst into tears and said he stole it from Hop the innkeeper.

So Digory and Enid followed the King's trail to the edge of the village and a down-at-the heels tavern called the No One Inn.

Funny Little Habits . . .

Clutching her father's burned, muddy cloak, Enid went inside to find Hop the innkeeper, while Digory took Barley and Pounce around the back to the tavern stable for a drink of water.

As Digory waited for Enid, the delicious smell of rabbit stew wafted toward him from the cottage next door. *Maybe there's a little extra in the pot for a hungry prince*, thought Digory hopefully, and he slipped off to find out.

While he was gone, Barley spotted a feedbag of hay hanging at the back of the stable. *Maybe there's a little extra in the bag for a hungry horse*, she thought . . .

Just as Digory sat down at the kind neighbor's table for a bowl of stew, a cry of panic rang out.

"FIRE! FIRE! THE STABLE'S ON FIRE!"

Digory leaped to his feet—it had to be Pounce! He ran to the tavern just in time to see a huge, angry innkeeper, with muscles like pumpkins, run out with a pitchfork.

"Who set my stable on fire?" Hop roared. "I'll have his guts for garters!"

Digory looked around. A small, scorched green tail was slithering into the woods.

"Hey, you there . . . suspicious stranger!" the innkeeper thundered. Digory decided it was not the moment to make friends. He dived into the woods and scrambled after Barley and Pounce as fast as his jelly legs would carry him.

ALL IS LOST!

Digory kept running through the bushes and brambles until he could no longer hear the innkeeper's shouts. Then he stopped to catch his breath. *Where was Enid? Why hadn't she come back?*

Pounce licked his nose, as if she knew she'd done something wrong. Her sooty breath made Digory feel very guilty. Through the trees he could see sparks flying from the burning stable. "It's not your fault, Pounce." He stroked her scaly forehead. "I shouldn't have left you. And I shouldn't have run away."

Although King Widget had never given Digory a list of things princes were supposed to do, Digory was certain that they *weren't* supposed to run away. Or at least, the good ones weren't. He felt very bad indeed. (But would *you* have risked a stab from Hop's pitchfork?) How could he make things right again? *I know—I'll try the magic sword*, he thought. *If the sword can* make *fire, maybe it can put fire out. I could creep back to the stable secretly . . .*

He reached for the sword—but it wasn't hanging from his belt. He'd left it in the stable!

Poor Digory felt hopeless. Now the sword was lost, the King was lost, and Enid was lost too. *Who or what will be next?* he thought.

As Digory wondered what to do, he realized the answer to his own question—he was lost himself because Enid had the map!

Digory was flummoxed. He just didn't know what to do next. He pulled some apples out of the saddlebag and the three lost friends munched gloomily together. What chance was there now of finding the King? Digory had promised the Queen he wouldn't return without him. He wished with all his heart that Enid was there with one of her good ideas. Digory remembered her advice at the joust: Just pretend. *Maybe it's worth a try again*, he thought. So he shut his eyes and pretended she was right there beside him, eating an apple too.

"What should I do now?" asked Digory.

"Stick to our plan and look for the King," said the pretend Enid.

"But where should I look?" asked Digory.

"At Claggyboot Castle," said the pretend Enid, spitting out an apple seed.

"How will I find it without the map?" asked Digory.

"Ask that old man collecting acorns over there . . . ," said the pretend Enid and, licking her juicy fingers, she disappeared.

Chapter Six

DIRECTIONS

THE old man collecting acorns directed Digory to a winding road that took him out of the woods and along the riverbank.

Digory was much happier. He felt Enid was with him somehow, although he had no real idea where she was. As always, her advice seemed right. *After all*, Digory told himself, *you can only rescue one person at a time.* Maybe Enid went off because she'd caught sight of the King. Maybe they would both be waiting for him at Claggyboot Castle . . .

As the day went on, little Pounce, who was still so new, began to feel tired and dawdled behind. Barley kept waiting patiently for her to catch up and eventually nudged her in front, so she could give her an encouraging nuzzle every now and then.

Digory looked out for signposts to the castle. There were plenty of milestones along the way, but not one of them mentioned Claggyboot. They only marked the distance back to the No One Inn or forward to Warlock's Haunt—neither of which Digory wanted to visit. Still, the acorn man had seemed certain enough when he pointed in this direction.

"I expect it's just around the next bend," Digory promised weary Pounce.

Well, of course it wasn't. Did you guess? However, there was a little chapel with a Digory-length bench on the porch. It seemed the perfect place to rest. While Barley and Pounce nestled together on the grass nearby, Digory stretched out and had a nap.

If only he had gone *inside,* he might have found someone familiar, also taking a rest . . .

Refreshed and eager to continue his search, Digory left the chapel and carried on along the road.

Five miles to Warlock's Haunt. On they went.

Four miles to Warlock's Haunt. On they went.

Three miles to Warlock's Haunt. When would they find a sign for Claggyboot? *If I'm having trouble finding it,* Digory wondered, *how did King Widget manage? Did the King even remember where he was going at all?*

Once more the little dragon grew tired. Digory found a shady bank beneath a bridge, and they stopped for another rest.

If only Digory had rested *beside* the bridge, he might have met someone familiar walking across . . .

Again they went on. A pie man came whistling down the lane. Digory always had a pie-shaped space inside, hoping to be filled.

"Three apple pies for my horse, please," said Digory, "two for my . . . er . . . other horse, and two for myself. One for now and one for later," he added, not wanting to appear greedy.

The pie man shook his head sadly. "You just missed the last one, I'm afraid," he said. "Sold it to a young maiden."

Digory sighed. Three tummies rumbled emptily.

"But you'll find plenty of food for your-self and your horses over the hill," said the pie man kindly. "They're having a mudfling-ing match today."

Digory thanked him. "And have you seen a lost king wandering this way?" he asked.

"No, not this week," said the pie man, shaking his head. "I've seen a runaway cart-wheel, a dog with a string of sausages, and a giant eagle. But, sorry, no kings."

Digory tramped on over the hill and saw before him a castle surrounded by muddy fields. Not a pretty place to live, but the per-fect spot for a great clod-splattering, splurge-wallowing mudfling.

Sure enough, the tournament had begun, and a great crowd gathered to watch and cheer the teams. There were stalls selling caramel apples and cotton candy, and a roasted hog crackled on a spit.

With a giddy-up from Digory, Barley slipped and skidded down the hill as Pounce slid along behind her.

Pounce whinnied with excitement, setting

fire to a mud-smeared sign as she tumbled past. Unnoticed, "WARLOCK'S HAUNT—KEEP OUT!" was reduced to a pile of cinders.

Chapter Seven

REUNITED!

A T the tournament, Digory soon ate his fill of delicious treats. He was quite eager to hang around and watch a few fistfuls of the match, but he knew the Queen was desperately waiting for news of King Widget. "I'm afraid there's no time to lose, old friend," he said to Barley. "We must find our way to Claggyboot Castle." Barley, already so mud-splattered that she looked like a dappled pony, didn't seem to object.

Before he took a step, however, Digory heard a familiar, spine-chilling sound.

"Aaaarahaieeeeee!"

"What teams are playing?" he asked a boy at the back of the crowd.

"It's the Filthy Wenches versus the Mucky Maidens," said the boy.

The Mucky Maidens—his sister, Ethelburg's team! And if Digory was not mistaken, that was her second-best war cry, only slightly less fierce than her Captain's rally.

"HHUUURGHARAAAAAAAAGH!!!"

That was the one. The crowd went wild. Digory climbed onto Barley to get a look. A twenty-armed, twenty-legged mud monster squirmed and struggled in the middle of the pitch. Digory could just make out the figure of Ethelburg drenched in a slurry of gloop. Then, to his amazement, he spotted Enid in the crowd!

"Enid!" he shouted. But the cheering drowned his voice. Digory jumped down and tried to edge his way toward her through the excited throng, but it was impossible to push through. No matter how hard he tried, he found himself shoved to the back, where he suddenly stopped in disbelief—for there he saw King Widget himself, standing on a milking stool, licking a caramel apple, and watching the match!

OH HAPPY DAY!

Digory couldn't believe his eyes—the King safe, Enid found, and Ethelburg thrilling the crowd!

"Make way, let me through," he cried. "I must get to the—"

SPLAT! A giant glob of mud spun over the heads of the cheering spectators and knocked poor Digory out.

Chapter Eight

WARLOCK'S HAUNT

WHEN Digory came to, he was in a dim, damp dungeon.
"Where am I?" he said. "And *who* am I?"
Oh dear . . .

Sir Fearless

Digory had completely lost his memory.

He looked around in bewilderment. After some thought, he decided there were only two things he could be sure of. First, he was definitely in a dungeon; and second, he was definitely in trouble.

Digory examined his surroundings. Previous inhabitants had scratched messages on the walls such as "*I didn't do it, really*," and "*Home sweet home.*" Neither of these cheered him up much. There was one small, dirty broken window, but it was too high to reach. The only sounds he could hear outside were angry geese and creaky cartwheels.

Maybe my clothes will tell me who I am, he thought. Digory rifled through his pockets, but they had been expertly picked by a scoundrel in the crowd at the mudflinging match and were quite empty. He studied his clothes. They looked as though they'd been

out in the rain, slept in, and covered with mud. *So*, he concluded, *I'm someone without a penny in the world, who sleeps in his clothes and lives in a muddy place. That doesn't sound like a good life.* He sighed. *Maybe I'm better off in a dungeon after all.*

Poor Digory. He couldn't even remember Enid's smiling face to lift his spirits.

For two days and nights Digory was kept in the dungeon, with nothing but a straw mattress and a brown mouse for company.

The only person he saw was an old man who brought him food and drink. The dungeon keeper wasn't allowed to talk to Digory; in fact he seemed quite afraid of him and shuffled nervously away as soon as his duties were done.

On the third day, Digory was brought before Sir Fearless, the Lord of the Castle. A crowd had gathered in the great hall.

"Where am I?" Digory said, blinking in the light. "And, er . . . *who* am I?"

As he spoke everyone in the room hushed.

"He's lost his memory," whispered a little boy.

"Shh. It's only a trick," hissed his father.

"You are a prisoner at Warlock's Haunt," said Sir Fearless sternly. "And we know you are a wizard!"

"A *wizard*!" Digory was amazed. He tried out this thought in his head but it didn't seem familiar. "Are you sure?"

"We know you are a wizard because you traveled here with a dragon," said Sir Fearless. "And only wizards can tame dragons."

"A *dragon*!" gasped Digory. "Did I really?"

"Indeed," said Sir Fearless. "A small one," he added.

"But why am I a prisoner?" asked Digory the Wizard.

"Long ago, our King upset a powerful wizard, who came to this castle in disguise," said Sir Fearless. "So the wizard put a spell on him and made him disappear—right there, on that throne! No one has dared sit on it since."

He frowned. "It was a sad day and a terrible nuisance. I am only his second cousin once removed on his mother's side, but there was nobody else to rule the land." Sir Fearless sighed deeply. "Fishing is really my thing, you know," he said. "Anyway, since then wizards have been forbidden to come here. We changed the name of the castle to scare them off, but it obviously hasn't worked."

Digory felt sorry for Sir Fearless. Somewhere, in the back of his mind, he did remember fishing, and it seemed a happy thought.

"If I *am* a wizard," he said, "maybe I can think of a spell to bring your king back again?"

Sir Fearless considered this. "How do I know I can trust you?" he said. "You might turn me into a newt."

Digory could see his point of view. *How could he even trust himself*, he wondered.

"No," said Sir Fearless with a heavy heart. "You're quite small for a wizard and don't

seem like much trouble, but I can't see what
else to do except have your head chopped off."

Chapter Nine

DIGORY IN DANGER

BEFORE Digory had a chance to protest, faint, or run away, the old dungeon keeper came running into the great hall crying, "FIRE! FIRE! THE STABLE'S ON FIRE!"

"It's that dragon!" groaned Sir Fearless. "Take the wizard back to the dungeon.

Everyone else, grab a bucket and follow me to the well. I'll have *both* their heads chopped off tomorrow. What I'd give for a quiet day of fishing!"

Back in his dungeon, Digory, believing himself to be a wizard, tried some spells to get himself out of trouble. As he was used to composing songs and poems, Digory found he could make up spells quite easily.

"Change my size and change my shape—
Through this keyhole I'll escape!

Cold as ice and hot as mustard,
Turn these stone walls into custard!

Down the well all axes drop,
Save this wizard from the chop!"

The spells were not very good (but then, neither were his poems), and none of them worked.

"Something's missing," pondered Digory. That something, of course, was a wizard.

It seemed that Digory was destined for the chopping block in the morning. He rattled his well-locked door and searched for a loose stone or secret tunnel in the dungeon, but there was no escape.

Once more he was left with a last, unlikely hope that he'd wake up and find it had all been a bad dream.

Digory did wake up in the middle of the night, but he was still in the dungeon. Something hard and heavy had been pushed through the window and hit him on the head.

"Oddsboddikins!" he cried, jumping up. "What was that? What am I doing here?" The well-aimed blow had not just given him a bump—it had given him his memory back!

For a long while Digory sat and thought about everything that had happened since he'd arrived at the mudflinging match.

He could patch together some of it, like a jigsaw puzzle with missing pieces, but the whole picture wasn't clear. Some things just didn't make sense.

Digory felt around for what had hit him. In the darkness he cut his finger on the blade of a sword. Why, that could have killed him with one blow! He looked up at the high dungeon window. Who could have tried to kill him in the night? *They really don't like wizards around here at all*, he thought.

Still, a sword would be useful in getting out of his predicament. Digory picked it up. Tied around the handle was a note. He held it up to a thin shaft of moonlight and read the message on it.

Dear Digory,
Use this to get yourself out of trouble,
then meet me on the drawbridge.

    Enid x

Enid was there, at the castle! So it was the *magic* sword! Digory's spirits rose.

Immediately he pointed the sword at the dungeon door. After the usual delay, it swung open with a creak. Digory rushed out and promptly fell on his face.

"Ouch!" he cried.

"Ouch!" cried the bundle of rags he had tripped over. It was the dungeon keeper, trying to get some sleep. With great apologies, Digory took the torch from the wall and helped the old man to his feet. Then his mouth dropped open—for that old man dressed in rags was none other than King Widget himself!

"Your Majesty!" gasped Digory.

"Ah, yes!" said the King, sitting on the stone

step. "Thought you looked familiar, Diggers, my boy. Not the wizard type at all. Still, you can't be too careful with chaps disappearing and all that!"

Digory used his sword once more to provide the King with a new set of warm, dry clothes and, as the Queen had insisted, a clean handkerchief.

"How did you come to be in this dreadful place, Sire?" asked Digory. "The Queen was so worried when she couldn't find you."

"Silly old girl," chuckled the King. "Nothing to worry about. Just a bit of dungeon work—does a man good to do an honest day's work now and then. Mind you, I do miss the royal, um, you know . . . plumpy-feathersome-spring-'n'-bounce?"

"You miss your bed!" laughed Digory.

"Yes." The King laughed too. "A fellow gets a bit stiff sleeping on the floor. Not as young as I used to be, eh!"

Digory asked the King how he had come to be a dungeon keeper. The King explained, in his forgetful, muddled way, that he had gone up to the battlements at Widget Castle to watch the joust when a great giant eagle had swooped down and carried him off.

"Took me for miles in its enormous grabbers," the King said, wide-eyed.

"Claws," said Digory.

"Exactly," said the King. "My shiny ring-a-ding fell off . . ."

(*Crown*, guessed Digory.)

"My red roundabout fell off . . ."

(*Cloak*, guessed Digory.)

"Then I fell off, too. Bit of a drop, Diggers, but the fresh air did wonders for my sneezes, and I landed in, you know, yucky mucky goo."

"Mud, Your Majesty!"

"That's it. Then it began to pitter-patter," continued the King. "Along came Sir Scare-'em-off, riding back from his . . . oh . . . chase-the-antlers, and he brought me here to his castle."

"Why didn't he send for us to take you home?" said Digory.

"Well, you know my little problem, lad," said the King shyly. "Couldn't tell him where I came from or who I was. Couldn't remember that word . . ."

"King!" said Digory.

"That's the one. Must have it stitched onto my . . . um . . . arms-up, tuck-your-tail-in."

"Shirt."

"Yes," said King Widget. "Sharp thinking."

It seemed, however, that Sir Fearless had taken pity on the King and given him a hot meal and a job.

Now Digory told the King his news. "Enid is here, Your Majesty, waiting at the draw-bridge."

"Dear girl!" exclaimed the King. "Let's go at once."

But Digory persuaded the King to take a little detour on their way . . .

Chapter Ten

A LITTLE DETOUR . . .

As Digory and the King made their way silently through the courtyards and passages, Digory pondered further on what had happened.

Didn't a king disappear at Warlock's Haunt some time ago?

Didn't somebody say they'd changed the name of the castle?

They came to the great hall. Digory stood before the throne.

"Hurry up, Diggers," said King Widget impatiently. "Poor Enid's waiting on the up-and-over."

"I think somebody else is waiting for you too, Your Majesty," said Digory. He crossed his fingers for good luck and pointed the magic sword at the throne. Nothing. A bat fluttered in the rafters above. More nothing. *Maybe this needs wizard-strength magic?* thought Digory with disappointment.

Then, with a pop, as if he'd squeezed through a small invisible space, a royal figure appeared on the throne.

"Where's that tricky wizard?" said King Wortle, looking around. "Where did he go?"

"Wortle!" cried King Widget in astonishment. "Welcome back!" He threw his arms around his twin brother with delight.

King Wortle was completely baffled but happy indeed to see him.

"Where have you been all this time, eh?" asked King Widget. "You disappeared ten years ago."

King Wortle looked even more bamboozled. "Well, I don't know where I've been," he said, taking off his crown to scratch his head. "I've quite forgotten."

"Oh, don't worry, Worty," King Widget reassured him, "I forget things all the time. That's no problem, no problem at all."

Digory smiled to himself. It seemed that the twin brothers had much more than their identical looks in common.

There followed a whole confusion of explanation about wizards and rescues and mud and dungeons, with lots of laughter and misunderstanding. Digory explained how Sir Fearless had reluctantly ruled since King Wortle disappeared.

"*Sir Fearless*, you say?" muttered King Wortle. "I'm sure I don't have a relation with that name."

At that moment Sir Fearless, woken up by

all the noise, appeared in his nightshirt.

"Your Majesty!" he cried in astonishment.

"Herbert!" said the King.

It seemed that not only had the King's second cousin once removed changed the name of the castle to frighten off wizards—he'd changed his own name too.

Herbert was delighted to learn that his ruling days were over, but as long as he lived he never understood how a dungeon keeper became a king and a wizard became a prince.

Herbert was not the only one woken up by the celebration. One by one, the other inhabitants of the castle staggered in, yawning and complaining about the noise. However, before you could say "Long live the King," they were all clapping and cheering and dancing in their slippers around the throne.

Now Enid, sitting alone on the drawbridge, heard the rumpus and riot too. She crept across the dark courtyard, curious to see what was going on . . .

"Ouch!"

"Ouch!"

"Who's that?"

"It's me!"

Enid tweaked a long sausage nose. "Digory!" He had come to find her. They hugged each other.

"But what's all that noise?" asked Enid.

"Come and see . . ."

Enid couldn't believe her eyes. A jubilant crowd of people in their nightshirts were cavorting in the great hall, and in the middle was her father, King Widget, skipping like a schoolboy with his long-lost brother, Wortle!

What a reunion! Everything was explained all over again, with even more confusion and laughter. Enid added her story too. She told everyone how she'd lost Digory at the No One Inn because the bad-tempered innkeeper had spilled cider on her dress. By the time she'd mopped it dry, the stable had caught fire and Digory was nowhere to be seen. And she told them how she'd found the magic sword and made her own way to Warlock's Haunt by mistake, just like Digory.

"I always knew you weren't far away," said Digory.

The party went on until dawn. When nobody could dance another step, they raided the kitchen for a royal breakfast.

But at last Enid decided it was time to leave. "Mom will be so pleased to see you," she reminded King Widget as he wiped some egg from his whiskers.

And it really did seem time to go home for a happy ending . . .

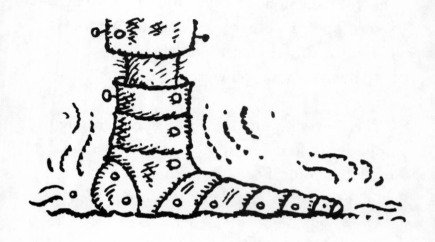

Chapter Eleven

ALMOST

JUST as Enid, Digory, and King Widget were saying their sleepy good-byes, everybody was shaken out of their boots and bedslippers by the most FEROCIOUS, EAR-SPLITTING ROAR!!

They all ran to the windows. An enormous fire-breathing dragon was stamping and

snorting flames on the other side of the moat.

The whole castle shook with panic.

Up went the drawbridge.

Out ran the archers, with their napkins still tucked into their nightshirts.

Onto the fire went big cauldrons of oil.

Anyone who had armor put it on.

Anyone who didn't grabbed a saucepan to put on his head.

Anyone without a saucepan hid under the bed.

Everybody panicked—except King Widget.

"Don't worry, Wortle," he said. "It's just a dragon. Digory can deal with those—no trouble at all. Done it a hundred times, haven't you, lad?" And he sat back down and helped himself to another buttered crumpet.

No Trouble at All?

Digory stared out of the window at the dragon. He gulped and shuddered. Although he had once been called Digory the Dragon Slayer, this was a name he'd acquired by mistake. He *had* once faced a dragon, it was true, but it turned out to have no teeth. Whereas this one had razor teeth and vicious claws and monstrous horns and frazzling flames and a very unfriendly look in its eye. Digory turned around for encouragement and support, but apart from King Widget having his second breakfast, there was no one to be seen. Even Enid was sitting under the table with a pudding bowl on her head. Digory clutched the

magic sword. Maybe this time there wouldn't be a happy ending after all . . .

ANOTHER REUNION?

The drawbridge was lowered and Prince Digory stepped forward to face the dragon. Once more in his desperate hour he remembered Enid's advice—just pretend. *But what should I pretend this time?* he wondered miserably. The dragon reared up and snarled, shooting a jet of flame high into the sky. Digory decided to pretend to be invisible . . .

Meanwhile, Barley hadn't stirred. Being deaf, she hadn't heard the midnight party or the roaring dragon. And as Barley hadn't stirred, Pounce hadn't stirred either. But now the smell of the dragon's fiery breath reached her nose. Pounce sniffed. The smoke smelled delicious . . .

As Digory took a step onto the drawbridge,

Pounce crept up shyly beside him, followed by Barley, who wasn't going to let her little one out of sight.

"That dragon's come for her baby," whispered a stable boy. The whisper went around the castle and, although he couldn't hear it, Digory was thinking the very same thought himself.

Barley looked up at the big dragon. Her four knobby knees began to knock in terror. She looked at Pounce, cowering now beside her. Then she looked at Digory.

Digory nodded sadly and Barley understood. She snuffled and licked her little one for the last time. Then, putting a brave hoof forward, she gently nudged Pounce onto the drawbridge. Everybody held their breath . . .

The big dragon peered down at Pounce, who trembled like a kitten. Slowly Digory began to step backward. He gestured to Barley to do the same, but, whether out of fear or love, the old carthorse wouldn't budge. Suddenly the big dragon curled its lip

and snarled. With a terrified whinny, Pounce turned tail and scuttled back to Barley.

Everybody gasped!

Now it was Barley's turn to snort and stamp her hoof as if to say, "What sort of mother does that?" Once more she pushed Pounce gently with her nose onto the drawbridge.

Once more everybody at Claggyboot Castle held their breath . . .

Pounce looked back, but Barley nodded her on. Nervously she stepped forward and gazed up into the glowering green eyes of the big dragon. For a moment she seemed mesmerized, but then she shook an invisible mane, turned tail, and scooted back to Barley.

"We're doomed!" everyone cried. "We'll all be fried and gobbled!"

"WHAT'S THE MEANING OF THIS?" the big dragon roared.

Everyone looked at Digory. Pretending to be invisible had definitely not worked. "It's not our f-f-fault," he stuttered. "We didn't steal her. She followed us. She thinks my h-h-horse is her m-m-mother . . ."

"I DON'T CARE ABOUT THAT!" bellowed the dragon. "IT'S GOT NOTHING TO DO WITH ME!"

"Haven't you come for your baby?" asked Digory.

"DO I LOOK LIKE THE MOTHERLY TYPE?" the dragon sneered. "I'VE COME FOR TREASURE AND ALL YOUR JUICY MAIDENS. AND I'LL ROAST YOUR SCRAWNY RIBS TOO, FOR GETTING IN MY WAY!"

At these loud and very clear words, Barley smartly pushed Pounce into the moat and jumped in after her!

Digory was left to face the dragon alone.

WHO'S CHICKEN?

Digory didn't need to pinch himself—he wasn't going to wake up from a dream. He knew there was no help to call on. He knew pretending wasn't going to work.

Then a voice from the castle shouted, "Come on, Diggers, do what you dragon slayers do. Time to get back to the grand-giggly-wimple."

Even at that dreadful moment, a smile crept onto Digory's face. King Widget believed he was a dragon slayer. King Widget had made him a prince. And although Digory didn't know what princes were supposed to do, he was certain they had to protect their kings.

Digory took a deep breath. He stepped forward, drew his sword, and pointed it at the dragon.

"I am Prince Digory, the Dragon Slayer. Be gone!" he cried.

The dragon stared in astonishment, then threw back its head and laughed a deep, thunderous, dragon-belly laugh that shook the ground beneath Digory's feet and made the drawbridge rattle.

"I'M NOT AFRAID OF A SQUIRMY

WORM LIKE YOU!" it roared. "I'LL TEAR THE STRINGY FLESH FROM YOUR SPINDLY BONES! I'LL . . . EURGH! . . . Awk! . . . cluck, cluck, cluck!"

With an explosion of scales and feathers, the dragon turned into a chicken.

"HOORAY!" The castle echoed with cheers of relief. "HOORAY FOR PRINCE DIGORY THE DRAGON SLAYER!"

Now it was Digory's turn to laugh as the dragon-chicken ran around in silly circles, squawking and snorting tiny puffs of black smoke from its beak. At the sound of its squawk a rooster strutted up, and before you could say "How-d'you-cock-a-doodle-do," that dragon-chicken ran off like the wind.

Barley and Pounce clambered, dripping, out of the moat.

"You're a good mother, Barley," said Digory, patting her mane. "When my hands stop shaking, I'll find you both a carrot." But in an instant Enid was there, with carrots and kisses and two happy kings.

"Well done, Diggers," said King Widget. "Funny foal you've got there—breed 'em with wings, eh? Young fellows these days," he chuckled, "full of new ideas."

"Thank you, Digory," said King Wortle, "from myself and all my kingdom. You deserve a great reward."

Digory shook his head bashfully. At that very moment he felt rewarded enough just to

119

be ungobbled. But King Wortle insisted on giving him the title of Royal Wizard of Claggyboot—and there was nothing Digory could say to change his mind.

THE UNFORGETTABLE DAY

"Now," said King Widget with a twinkle in his eye, "what day is it today?"

"It's our birthday!" cried King Wortle, who never forgot it either.

"Then I suggest we all go home to my um, you know . . . turrets-and-twirly-steps . . ."

"Castle," giggled Enid.

"On the tip of my tongue," said King Widget with a wink. "And we'll have a great birthday knees-up-and-hurdy-gurdy! Better still, we'll have a charge-and-thrust! Yes, a great birthday charge-and-thrust. Everyone is invited. Diggers can do the jousting. No problem for a fellow like him. Done it all before."

Enid looked at Prince Digory the Dragon

Slayer, Royal Wizard of Claggyboot, whose heart had just sunk into his cold tin boots. She tugged a lock of his red hair and grinned. "Don't worry," she whispered, "I'm sure a piglet race will do just as well!"

Digory smiled with relief. "Are you sure?"

Enid nodded.

"Then let's go home," said Digory. After all, it really *was* time for a happy ending . . .

A NOTE ON THE AUTHOR

Angela McAllister is the author of more than fifty books for children, several of which she has illustrated herself. Angela has two children who are fantastic bookworms and a brilliant inspiration. She lives with her family in a crumbly sixteenth-century cottage with an unruly garden in Hampshire, England. This is Angela's eighth book for Bloomsbury.

A Note on the Illustrator

Ian Beck is the author and illustrator of several books for children, including the picture book *Winston the Book Wolf* by Marni McGee. He lives in London with his wife and children.

Be sure to look for . . .

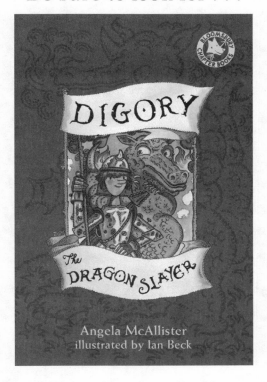

"Beck's rumpled drawings and vignettes add more amiably comic touches. Ready cheeks; insert tongues." —*Kirkus Reviews*

"In this affectionate send-up of heroic fantasy, Digory is a reluctant knight who gamely tries to live up to the role of dauntless hero, while Enid is a refreshingly independent princess. The amusing black-and-white drawings add to the mock-medieval fun. The lighthearted plot and the strong underlying message about courage and individuality make this a good choice for fantasy fans." —*SLJ*